Kaleidoscopic Design
Coloring Book

Lester Kubistal

DOVER PUBLICATIONS, INC.
Mineola, New York

Note

The kaleidoscope, an instrument invented in 1817, is usually made of mirrors and bits of colored glass. As you look into one end of the cylinder, you see dazzling, multi-colored patterns that are vibrant like stained glass and as intricate as mosaic-work, yet are perfectly symmetrical and precise in their shapes. These images have inspired countless graphic works and now you can create your own.

All of the drawings in this book were painstakingly crafted, free-hand and with no mechanical aids, by artist Lester Kubistal. Bring them to life by filling them with color, and you will enjoy many hours of challenging fun.

Bibliographical Note

Kaleidoscopic Design Coloring Book is a new work, first published by Dover Publications, Inc., in 1999.

DOVER *Pictorial Archive* SERIES

This book belongs to the Dover Pictorial Archive Series. You may use the designs and illustrations for graphics and crafts applications, free and without special permission, provided that you include no more than four in the same publication or project. (For permission for additional use, please write to: Permissions Department, Dover Publications, Inc., 31 East 2nd Street, Mineola, New York, 11501.)

However, republication or reproduction of any illustration by any other graphic service, whether it be in a book or in any other design resource, is strictly prohibited.

International Standard Book Number: 0-486-40566-4

Manufactured in the United States of America
Dover Publications, Inc., 31 East 2nd Street, Mineola, N.Y. 11501